Bits and Bites of Truth and Wisdom

Nathlee R. Grant

Published by Nathlee R. Grant, 2024.

BITS AND BITES OF TRUTH AND WISDOM

First edition. April 12, 2024.

ISBN: 979-8231874781

Written by Nathlee R. Grant.

Also by Nathlee R. Grant

Breaking Chains: A Mother's Journey to Healing and Redemption

Bits and Bites of Truth and Wisdom

Table of Contents

This book is dedicated to my children and grandchild, whose endless support and encouragement made it all possible.

BITS AND BITES

Of Truth and Wisdom

Nathlee R. Grant

Preface

THIS COMPILATION OF reflections takes readers on a spiritual journey, exploring themes of self-discovery, godly guidance, and purposeful living. It begins with an introspective examination of one's journey from personal limitations and delves into the ongoing process of shedding old habits and mindsets. These reflections emphasize the importance of aligning one's thoughts with God's divine perspective, as seen through the lens of Psalms 139:17-18, where God's boundless love and thoughts towards humanity are explored.

These reflections weave personal stories together illustrating a facet of spiritual growth and self-realization. From nurturing healthy relationships and embodying the fruits of the spirit to navigating life's storms with divine wisdom and finding clarity amidst temptation. These reflections offer insights into the transformative power of faith and surrender.

Furthermore, this compilation underscores the significance of embracing one's purpose and living in alignment with God's plan even amidst challenges and uncertainty. It encourages readers to cultivate an attitude of gratitude, trust, and compassion; recognizing the inherent trust God places in His creations and the responsibility to honour His divine breath within us.

Through introspection, prayer, and a commitment to living authentically, the narrative inspires readers to embark on their own journey of spiritual growth, trusting in God's guidance and embracing the abundant life He offers.

Word from the Author

> "Each breath becomes a sacred opportunity to praise the God of breath, to embody His love and grace in every aspect of my life"

WALKING WITH CHRIST, the risen saviour, and exploring the intricacies of my emotions and beliefs reminds me of the profound love and trust bestowed upon humanity by God. This journey extends beyond mere understanding and leans towards a deeper connection with His boundless love and grace.

Solace and inspiration are found in contemplating the sheer magnitude of God's thoughts towards us expressed so eloquently by the psalmist in Psalm: 139:17-18. As I reflect further I find His thoughts towards us are countless, like grains of sand on the shore, encompassing every aspect of our being. In moments of quiet reflection, I also find that there is humility in realizing that His love transcends flaws and shortcomings, embracing us in all our imperfections.

Yet, amidst this realization, I am confronted with this fundamental truth: God trusted humanity before we ever dared to trust Him. This notion resonates deeply, challenging individuals to reevaluate their relationship with Him. In my challenge I begin to ponder: how can

His trust be fully embraced and how can His faithfulness and grace be honoured?

As I delve deeper into the essence of divine trust, I find I am filled with a profound sense of purpose and duty. I then find that each breath becomes a sacred opportunity to praise the 'God of breath', embodying His love and grace in every aspect of life. This revelation calls us to action, the compelling action of aligning our thoughts with God's divine perspective.

I am cognisant, however, that there are daily challenges to confronting personal beliefs and emotions to cultivate a mindset that reflects His unconditional love and grace. Through introspection and prayer, though, there is a seeking to align our thoughts with His, by dwelling in the richness of His love and embracing His trust.

In sharing this reflection, there is an invitation for us to embrace divine trust together. Let us then ponder the depths of God's thoughts towards us, allowing His love to permeate every aspect of life. Together, let us cultivate a mindset of gratitude and grace, honouring His faithfulness and embracing His trust in us.

I pray that as we feast together on these tasty morsels of 'bits and bites' our lives will be filled to overflowing.

Through the Wilderness

Journeying Beyond Egypt

> "Our journey out of Egypt is not a one-time event but an ongoing process of shedding old habits and mindsets."

AS I PONDER ON BIBLICAL Egypt, I find it to be a land of oppression for the ancient Israelites. Beyond the physical shackles, however, was the stronghold the Egyptian culture still had on their minds. That culture was hard to shake off after 400 years of slavery and it has been used as symbol of captivating habits ever since. A little bit of Egypt resides within each of us, whether manifested as familiar comforts or the ignorance of alternatives. I then came to find that the journey of getting this culture out is ongoing and involves a continuous process of shedding old habits and changing mindsets. It resembles the 40 year wilderness experience the Israelites had to go through to rid themselves of Egypt. It was a journey requiring both introspection and outward action.

Fascinatingly I came to conclude that progress necessitates a defined destination, a goal beyond metaphorical Egypt. This progressive journey is fraught with surrounding ourselves with like-minded individuals and offers vital support and accountability as you strive for a better future, liberated from the chains of your past, together.

I go further to reiterate and recommend establishing boundaries and guidelines is also key to preventing regression, while seeking guidance and support helps us stay on course. Renewing our minds with scriptural wisdom and aligning ourselves with God's will facilitate breaking free from Egypt's grip.

I close with this reminder. This journey demands active participation. Yet, through surrender and guidance, we can gradually release Egypt's hold and step into a new, liberated existence. Let us approach this process with compassion for ourselves and others, understanding that true freedom awaits those who persevere.

Penny for your thought

- do you still feel the pull of 'Egypt,' in areas of your life?
- what steps can you take, both inwardly and outwardly, to move towards true freedom and alignment with God's will?

Journey of Self-Discovery

> “unvoiced emotions often led to anger, bitterness, and hatred, all stemming from a fear of vulnerability”

OVER SEVERAL MONTHS, I embarked on a transformative journey of self-discovery, stepping beyond my personal ‘Egypt’. This path began with the recognition of my struggle to effectively express my emotions. It became evident that while I could communicate my thoughts, my feelings often remained unspoken. For instance, I could easily say, “I think that person has a problem with me,” but I struggled to express how that situation made me feel.

These unvoiced emotions often led to anger, bitterness, and hatred, all stemming from a fear of vulnerability. I feared that being vulnerable would lead to being overlooked and hurt even more.

Yet, amidst this fear, I felt a stirring within—a call to embrace change. I knew deep down that transformation required me to confront my discomfort and practice vulnerability. Despite the uncertainty, I took courageous steps towards emotional expression, starting with trusted companions who offered support and understanding. This journey was challenging, but each small step brought profound rewards of healing and growth.

Reflection and Encouragement:

- ***Recognizing Emotions***: Acknowledging our emotions is the first step towards emotional freedom and healing.
- ***Courage in Vulnerability***: Embracing vulnerability allows us to connect authentically with ourselves and others.
- ***Trusting the Process***: Through perseverance and support, we can overcome fear and experience transformative change.

In this journey, I discovered that true freedom comes from facing our fears and embracing vulnerability. As I continue to grow, I am learning to express my emotions honestly and cultivate deeper, more meaningful relationships. May this journey inspire you to embrace your own path of self-discovery with courage and faith, knowing that each step brings you closer to wholeness and peace.

Penny for your thought

- In your own journey of self-discovery,
    - what fears or habits do you recognize as barriers to expressing your true self

Navigating the Path of Purpose

> "our purpose isn't just about what we do, but who we are becoming in Christ"

DISCOVERING ONE'S PURPOSE is indeed a journey filled with unexpected twists and turns. It's a path where we often find ourselves navigating through different roles and vocations, seeking that profound sense of fulfilment. Along this journey, there are moments of clarity that brighten our way, as well as moments of uncertainty that challenge our understanding of identity and calling. For the pursuit of the pursuit of true calling holds the key to unlocking potential and making a lasting impact

Reflecting on my own experiences, I recall times spent pursuing various avenues—whether in relationships or noble endeavours—always pondering how they aligned with my true purpose. It was a journey marked by trial and error, where I pushed forward with determination, yet often realized the need for realignment with God's purpose.

Scripture reminds us that our steps are ordered by the Lord, and that He has a unique plan for each of us (Psalm 37:23). This truth underscores the significance of seeking His guidance in discerning our purpose. For me, this meant surrendering my ambitions and desires to align more closely with God's intentions. It involved moments of deep introspection and prayer, seeking clarity and understanding in His word.

Through this process, I discovered that our purpose isn't just about what we do, but who we are becoming in Christ. It's about living out His will with faithfulness and integrity, allowing His light to shine through our lives. As I surrendered more fully to God's leading, I found peace and assurance in knowing that He directs my steps and equips me for His purposes.

Today, I encourage you to embrace your own journey of discovering purpose. Take time to reflect on how your experiences and aspirations align with God's plan for your life. Seek His guidance through prayer and study of His word, trusting that He will reveal His purpose and provide the wisdom and strength needed to fulfil it.

May this journey be a transformative experience, where you discover the joy of walking in God's purpose and experiencing His abundant blessings in your life.

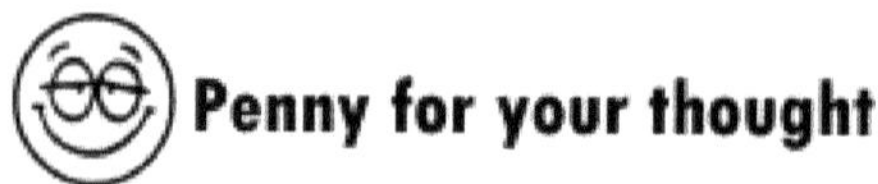

- How has prayer and studying God's word helped you in your journey of discovering and fulfilling your purpose?

- What advice would you give to someone who is struggling to discern their purpose? Based on your own experiences, what encouragement would you offer?

Navigating Life's Pushes with Purpose: Cultivating Divine Guidance

> "By tuning to His wisdom and seeking His direction, we can discern when to push forward and when to pause"

THE BIRTH OF NEW LIFE often involves enduring pain, a testament to perseverance. Indeed, without this effort without the unwavering determination to see it through, the miracle of birth would not unfold. Yet, it's essential to acknowledge that not all efforts are equal. There are moments when we find ourselves pushing against the tide, expending energy on endeavours that may not align with our true purpose.

In these instances, it becomes paramount to realign ourselves with the divine guidance of God. By tuning to His wisdom and seeking His direction, we can discern when to push forward and when to pause, when to exert our efforts on endeavours that truly matter and when to relinquish control and trust in His plan.

It's a delicate balance, navigating the currents of life with faith and perseverance, until finding that one which ultimately leads us closer to our purpose and fulfilment. As we journey onward, may we find solace in the knowledge that God's guidance is ever-present, guiding us along the path toward our true calling.

Penny for your thought

- Reflect on the balance between striving toward goals and surrendering to God's timing and plan. How do you maintain this balance in your life?

- How has tuning into God's wisdom and seeking His direction impacted your decision-making process? Be specific

Navigating Life's Storms with Divine Wisdom

> "Through the wisdom bestowed upon me by the spirit of God, I've come to understand that navigating life's challenges requires wisdom above all else."

IN MOMENTS WHEN LIFE'S tumultuous waves crash upon us, there's often a feeling of being overwhelmed. It proves futile to wrestle against such relentless tides. Reflecting on these experiences reveals the folly of attempting to compete with the raging sea.

The sea, much like life itself, has calm moments where little effort is needed. Yet, during these serene interludes, there's a risk of complacency, assuming tranquillity will always prevail. However, when the sea inevitably unleashes its fury, frustration and resentment can consume us.

It's important to recognize that our anger cannot overpower the mighty roar of life's tumultuous sea. With the wisdom bestowed by the spirit of God, we understand that navigating life's challenges requires wisdom above all else. Through wisdom, we can steer through its currents and weather its storms with resilience and grace.

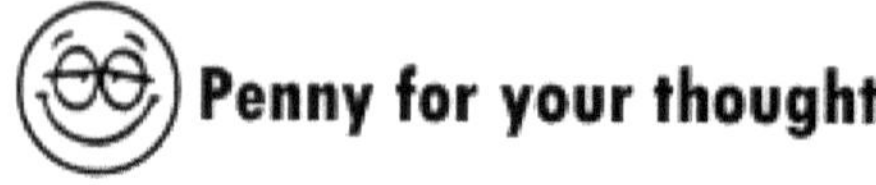

- In what ways can you cultivate the wisdom needed to navigate life's challenges with resilience and grace, recognizing that anger and frustration are futile against the mighty forces of the sea?

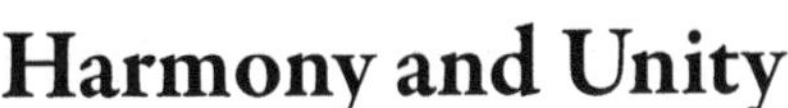

Harmony and Unity

BITS of Wisdom

Fostering Harmony: The Essential Role of the Fruit of the Spirit in Relationships

> "the absence of kindness, compassion, and love corrodes the very fabric of relationships, leading to discord and conflict."

THE SIGNIFICANCE OF cultivating the fruit of the spirit is paramount in fostering healthy relationships. It is a profound reflection on why these virtues are not merely personal attributes, but essential elements in our interactions with others. When we ponder upon the fruits of love, patience, kindness, goodness, and long-suffering, we realize their pivotal role in the dynamics of human connection.

Consider the essence of these virtues: they serve as the bedrock upon which relationships flourish. Without them, relationships falter, crumble, and ultimately disintegrate. It is the embodiment of these qualities that allows us to navigate the complexities of human interaction with grace and understanding.

Indeed, the absence of kindness, compassion, and love corrodes the very fabric of relationships, leading to discord and conflict. It is no wonder that the world is plagued by strife when individuals lack the spiritual nourishment necessary to coexist harmoniously.

The manifestation of the fruit of the spirit is not merely about personal virtue or salvation; it is about exemplifying the divine qualities inherent within us. By embracing these virtues, we not only enrich our own lives but also contribute to the creation of a more compassionate and empathetic society.

In essence, cultivating the fruit of the spirit is not a solitary endeavour aimed at personal righteousness. Rather, it is a communal effort to embody the divine qualities that facilitate meaningful and enduring relationships. It is through the manifestation of these virtues that we foster unity, understanding, and harmony in our interactions, thereby reflecting the very essence of Godliness in our engagement with one another.

Penny for your thought

- Can you actively cultivate the fruits of the spirit—love, patience, kindness, goodness, and long-suffering—in your interactions with others, contributing to a more compassionate and empathetic society?

Embracing Divine Grace: A Journey of Gratitude, Surrender, and Abundance

> "Acknowledging my reliance on God's providence, I find solace in surrendering control and trusting in the wisdom of His plan"

REFLECTING ON THE GRACE and love of God evokes profound gratitude and humility. Without His guiding presence, one can only wonder where life might lead. There is a deep sense of thankfulness for His unwavering support and guidance, without which one would be adrift in uncertainty.

Acknowledging reliance on God's providence, there is solace in surrendering control and trusting in the wisdom of His plan. This relinquishment brings peace and freedom, allowing navigation of life's complexities with a lighter heart.

In this state of surrender, the burden of scarcity fades, replaced by a deep sense of abundance. Freed from fear and insecurity, one is empowered to share generously, knowing that what is possessed is always sufficient. This attitude fosters responsibility and gratitude, nurturing the cherishing and stewardship of entrusted blessings.

Ultimately, it is through this profound connection with God that purpose, fulfilment, and the capacity to live a life guided by love, gratitude, and compassion are found.

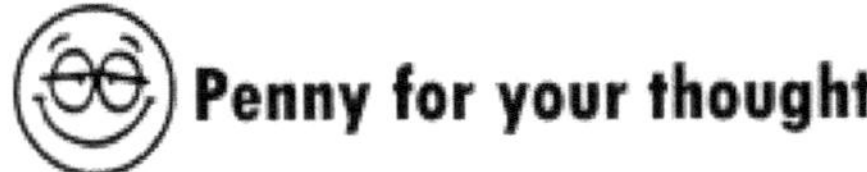

- What does surrendering to God looks like to you practically?
- How can you cultivate a deeper sense of surrender and trust in God's plan, allowing His guidance to lead you through life's uncertainties with peace and freedom?

God's Sovereignty

BITS of Wisdom

Faith in God's Plan: Trusting His Best for Us

> "when circumstances seem bleak and harmful, trust in the Lord, for His plans are to prosper you and not to harm you"

RELY ON THE LORD ALWAYS, knowing that He has your best interests at heart and in His hand. God's love for His children ensures that the best outcomes are guaranteed. However, our perception of what is best often falls short of God's divine plan, leading us into confusion and discouragement.

Even when circumstances seem bleak and harmful, trust in the Lord, for His plans are to prosper you and not to harm you. Remember, God has promised never to leave nor forsake us, so when situations appear contrary to this promise, hold steadfast in your trust.

In fact, your purpose in life will be fulfilled according to His design. Therefore, we must prioritize believing in God's best over our own limited understanding.

Penny for your thought

- How can you deepen your trust in God's plans, even when they may seem contrary to your own expectations or understanding,

- Do you believe that God's love and wisdom surpasses all your expectations or understanding?

God's Supremacy Over Pain

> God's power surpasses any pain we may endure,

UNTIL RECENTLY, I HADN'T fully grasped the significance of the statement, "God is bigger than your pain." Despite declaring God as the Almighty in various situations, I hadn't specifically considered His supremacy over pain. However, on the evening of October 28, 2018, after experiencing excruciating pain, I came to recognize the truth in this assertion.

The pain I endured that evening was intense, starting from my abdomen and radiating towards sensitive areas. It immobilized me, leaving me unable to move. Yet, amidst this agony, I chose to magnify God above all else. I recalled past instances of pain, realizing that tensing up only intensified the discomfort. Instead, I focused on controlled breathing, which brought calmness and peace, even healing.

Encouraged by my experience, I shared this breathing technique with others facing similar pain. I recounted my journey of healing through reliance on God's grace, urging them to surrender their pain to Him. Recently, when confronted with severe pain myself, I had a choice: surrender to it or invite God into the midst of it. Remembering my commitment to serve Christ alone, I chose to worship Him, acknowledging His sovereignty overall, including pain.

In moments of agony, I declare, "God is bigger than this!" Drawing strength from Psalms 25:15, I keep my eyes fixed on the Lord, trusting Him to deliver me from the snares of pain and affliction. Indeed, God's power surpasses any pain we may endure, offering solace and strength in our times of need.

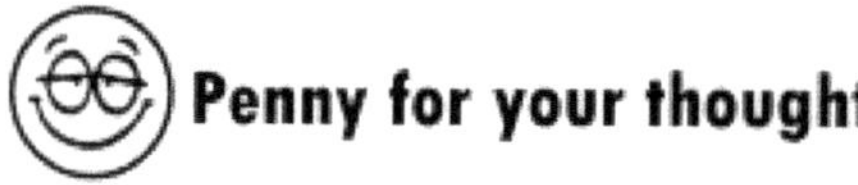

- Do you find it easy entrusting your pain to God?
- Do you rely on God's capacity to bring healing and deliverance to you amidst suffering?

Breath of Trust

> God trusted us before we ever dared to trust Him!

AS I REFLECT ON THE boundless goodness of God, a profound realization dawns upon me: the unwavering trust He places in us, His creations. In moments of quiet contemplation, I find myself enveloped in the sheer faithfulness of God – a faithfulness that transcends time and circumstance. It is in these moments of basking in His faithfulness that I am granted a revelation of profound trust, a trust so pure and unwavering that it leaves me awe-struck.

As I delve deeper into the essence of this trust, I am reminded of the fundamental truth that God trusted us before we ever dared to trust Him. The scriptures proclaim that we love because He first loved us crafting us in His likeness and breathing life into our very beings. It is this act of divine trust that leaves me humbled, for it is an acknowledgment of the sacred responsibility entrusted to us by the Creator Himself.

The realization of God's breath coursing through my veins fills me with a sense of purpose and duty. Each inhalation, each exhalation is not merely a biological function but a sacred opportunity to praise the God of breath, the one who bestowed upon me the gift of life itself. In this moment of revelation, I am compelled to ask myself: How am I utilizing this precious gift of breath? Am I honouring God's trust in me by using it to uplift and glorify His name?

With a newfound awareness of the divine trust placed upon me, I am called to action. Let everything that has breath praise the Lord – a proclamation that resonates deeply within my soul. My breath, infused with the very essence of God, becomes a vessel for worship and praise, a testament to His unending grace and boundless love.

In sharing this revelation, I implore you to consider the weight of God's trust in you. Are you using the breath of God bestowed upon you to its fullest potential? Let us join together in praise and adoration, honouring the God of breath which entrusted to us, the gift of life itself.

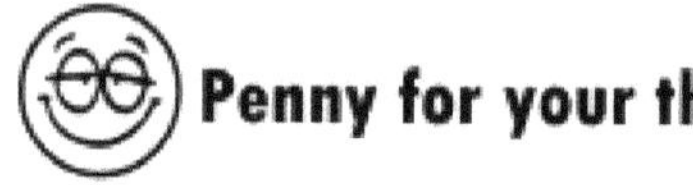

- In what moments do you notice yourself utilizing the breath of God in ways that fail to honor Him?

- how can you redirect those moments to align with His divine purpose?

Holding Fast to God's Plans

> "In patience and prayer, find solace, for He is always on time."

IN THE SACRED JOURNEY of life, we often find ourselves at crossroads where the path of compromise beckons us with its enticing promises. It whispers sweet lies of convenience, promising quick fixes and temporary satisfaction. But in these moments, we must remember the steadfastness of our faith, the unwavering strength found in God.

The enemy, in various guises—be it situations that challenge our resolve, fear that paralyzes our steps, anger that clouds our judgment, or greed that taints our intentions—tempts us to veer off the path of righteousness. It seeks to ensnare us in its grasp, to negotiate away our values and principles, thus tying the hands of God and compromising His divine plans for us.

Reflect upon the tale of David and Bathsheba, a narrative charged with the consequences of compromise. Amidst the shadows of temptation, David faltered, succumbing to the allure of desire. Yet, even in his transgression, God's will prevailed. Solomon, their son, was ordained to build the temple of the Almighty, a testament to divine providence amidst human frailty.

The repercussions of compromise are manifold, woven into the fabric of our existence. They bring naught but loss, disgrace, and anguish. Negotiations with the enemy lead only to a shifting of the sands, where plans are altered, and God's sovereignty is supplanted by the will of man.

In the aftermath of compromise, David found himself entangled in a web of deceit, orchestrating Uriah's fate to align with his own desires. Yet, even in the darkest of hours, there is hope. For God is ever watchful, His timing impeccable.

As we navigate the tempests of life, let us remain steadfast in prayer, trusting in His divine timing. Do not falter, dear pilgrim, in the face of compromise. Guard your heart against the wiles of the enemy, for God's plans are immutable, His promises unyielding. In patience and prayer, find solace, for He is always on time.

Penny for your thought

IN LIFE'S SACRED JOURNEY, we encounter tempting crossroads where compromise seems all too easy.

- How can we remain steadfast in our faith, resisting the magnetism of convenience and ensuring that God's divine plans for us prevail over the whispers of compromise?

Finding Clarity Amidst Temptation

> "Recognizing God's divine grace eliminates the temptation to misinterpret situations and attribute incorrect meanings."

WHEN I AM MINDFUL OF God's omnipresence and His encompassing nature, my perception of myself and the situations around me undergoes a profound shift.

Conversely, when I neglect this awareness, I find myself in constant inner turmoil. For instance, imagine a scenario where someone of the opposite sex shows kindness towards you. Upon receiving their gesture with gratitude, you suddenly find yourself questioning whether you harbour romantic feelings for them. In truth, what you truly desire is to always be treated kindly by this person. However, if they were to deny you that kindness or withdraw it, you spiral into guilt and rejection.

What unfolds in such instances is the sway of desire and a distorted perception, far removed from reality. Only acknowledging the truth can emancipate us from this cycle. So, where does God fit into all of this? From the outset, when the person treated you kindly, it was God's grace working through them. Recognizing God's divine grace eliminates the temptation to misinterpret situations and attribute incorrect meanings.

Therefore, by embracing God's grace, we dispel the illusions that lead us astray and open ourselves to a clearer understanding of reality.

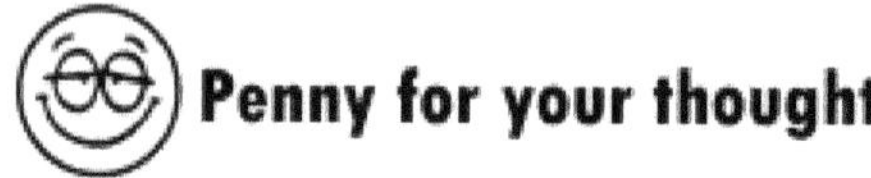

- How can we cultivate a deeper awareness of God's presence in our daily interactions, freeing ourselves from the distortions of desire and embracing a clearer understanding of reality?

Become Christ-Like

Inviting Jesus In: Surrendering to Him

> "Surrendering ourselves entirely to Him is not easy; it often involves admitting our faults and acknowledging that we've been handling things incorrectly."

I VISUALISE THE LORD gently knocking at the doors of our hearts. With the doors partially open, we cautiously peer out and inquire, "Who is it?" "It's me," responds Jesus. "I am Jesus. May I come in?"

Some of us hesitate, citing the untidiness of our room, asking for time to tidy up before inviting Him in. We promise to call once everything is in order. Others inquire about the duration of His stay, seeking to manage His presence. There are those who invite Jesus in but insist on showing Him where He'll stay, attempting to maintain some control over the situation.

Yet, for Jesus to truly fill us, He must take over. For His light to shine through us, He must inhabit us completely. This requires us to let Him in willingly, granting Him permission to dwell within our hearts. Surrendering ourselves entirely to Him is not easy; it often involves admitting our faults and acknowledging that we've been handling things incorrectly.

However, it is through this surrender that transformation occurs. It's a process of relinquishing control and allowing Jesus to guide our lives. Only then can His light illuminate our being, radiating through us to the world around us.

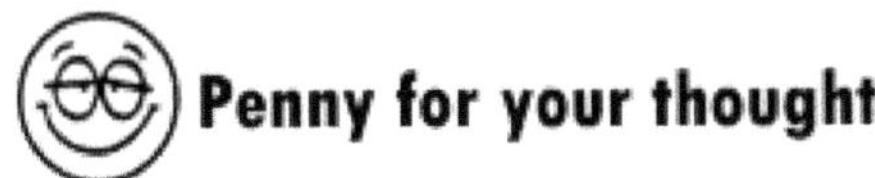

- How can you move beyond hesitation and surrender fully to Jesus, allowing His light to shine through you?
- What are you afraid to show Jesus?

Living Like Christ: Embracing Love, Justice, and Abundant Life

> We no longer need to cling to survival instincts; instead, we can embrace abundant life

"FOR OUR STRUGGLE IS not against flesh and blood, but against the rulers, against the authorities, against the powers of this dark world and against the spiritual forces of evil in the heavenly realms." - Ephesians 6:12.

Often, we find ourselves grappling not only with the issues we despise but also with the individuals involved. It can be challenging to separate the person from their beliefs or positions, especially when they are deeply entrenched in their convictions. I've caught myself referring to them as the problem itself, which only fuels my frustration towards them, ultimately hindering any resolution.

This approach leads to a lose-lose situation, where neither side gains ground, and the real adversary, the enemy of our souls, triumphs. Engaging in quarrelsome debates about issues rarely leads to solutions in our culture. To effect meaningful change and address issues at their core, we must approach them with deliberation, discerning what actions to take.

This is where the example of Christ becomes paramount. Jesus of Nazareth walked the earth embodying the attributes of God the Father. He taught and demonstrated that through love, we can overcome and transform cultures. Love was at the core of His being, motivating Him to protect our dignity and address the issues we faced.

Upon reflecting on these truths, I realized that Christ died so that we might truly live. We no longer need to cling to survival instincts; instead, we can embrace abundant life. As 2 Corinthians 5:17 states, in Christ, we become new creations, old things passing away, and all things becoming new.

Living justly and abundantly reflects our belief in Christ's sacrifice for us. Rather than merely surviving, we can show others the richness of life by embodying the life of Christ within us. It is through living like Christ that we draw others to the source of life. We are the tangible representation of Christ in the world, and our lives should reflect His life-giving love to all.

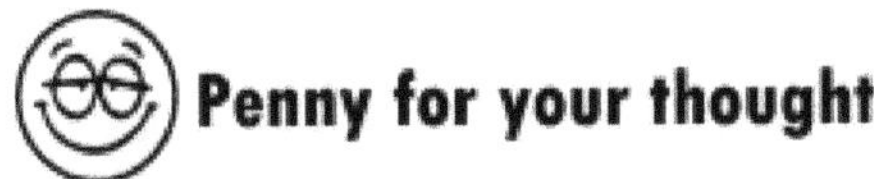

- Are you living in the abundance of Christ?
- How easy is it for you to look beyond someone's fault and see the need?

Embracing the Purpose of Giving

> "Giving transcends mere action; it emanates from the core of our being"

GOD DOESN'T DESIRE our weariness; He seeks our emptiness. This profound notion emphasizes a shift in perspective from fatigue to fulfilment. The concept pivots on the idea that our purpose lies not in exhaustion but in the richness of what we pour out.

Consider the significance of what you offer. The essence of your being is reflected not in idle potential but in active contribution. The operative word, therefore, is "give." It is through the act of giving that we truly reveal ourselves, showcasing our generosity and the depth of our character. Quantity matters, for it speaks volumes about our capacity to give from the abundance of our hearts.

Let's delve deeper into this analogy using a simple container, like a bottle of water. This vessel holds myriad possibilities within its confines. Yet, its true utility is realized only when its contents are poured forth. Without dispensing water, its potential remains untapped. Similarly, our lives hold boundless potential, but we achieve true significance when we are willing to give of ourselves repeatedly, replenishing our capacity to serve others.

Giving transcends mere action; it emanates from the core of our being. It's not merely about doing but about the heartfelt ability to act with compassion and selflessness. Understanding who we are entails recognizing our capacity to give, a reflection of our innate purpose.

In this analogy, God is likened to a source waiting to pour out blessings upon us. Like a refillable pen, we are meant to be vessels ready to be reused, to be filled again and again with divine grace and purpose.

What we give is emblematic of our belief. Just as a pen is designed to be used for writing, so are we fashioned to fulfil a specific purpose. Our value lies not in the multiplicity of tasks we can perform but, in our willingness, to pour out what we contain within us.

Consider the pen. Its utility is contingent upon the ink it holds within. Likewise, our worth is tied to the substance we carry within our souls, ready to spill out in acts of kindness, love, and service. Without this inner essence, our potential remains unrealized, our purpose unfulfilled.

Penny for your thought

- What motivate you to give?
- how can you ensure that what you pour out reflects the essence of your souls and fulfills your divine purpose?

Unravelling Anger

> "anger, contrary to popular belief, isn't merely a feeling but rather a state we find ourselves in because of a feeling."

I'M STARTING TO REALIZE that anger, contrary to popular belief, isn't merely a feeling but rather a state we find ourselves in because of a feeling. This realization came to me when I received a message that triggered a surge of rage within me.

As I found myself consumed by this intense emotion, I began to examine my feelings more closely. It was perplexing because my reactions were inconsistent with my usual demeanour. Despite trying to identify the exact emotion I was experiencing, none of the familiar feelings seemed to match the turmoil in my heart. Eventually, I recognized that what I was feeling was a sense of being "set up" – a feeling of being deceived or manipulated.

Seeking guidance, I paused to pray, asking God to help me discern my emotions. In that moment of reflection, clarity emerged. I realized that acknowledging my feeling of being "set up" shifted my perspective and diffused the anger within me. It prompted me to contemplate what I truly wanted to do, leading me towards calmer and more constructive actions.

This experience led me to ponder whether anger is indeed a state we enter when we feel helpless. I noticed that whenever I perceived a sense of empowerment or clarity, my anger subsided, replaced by a desire to respond with kindness and understanding.

Recognizing the potential for misunderstanding or differing perspectives, I resolved to express my point of view calmly and respectfully. Moving forward, I aim to introspect and examine the states I enter when feeling misunderstood, striving to respond with grace and clarity rather than succumbing to anger.

Penny for your thought

- How aware are you of the underlying emotions that trigger your anger,

- Do you find it easy to respond with grace and clarity than allowing anger to dictate our actions, especially in moments when you are feeling misunderstood or deceived?

Cultivating Inner Peace

> "This peace isn't just a calm exterior; it's a profound inner tranquillity ."

LIFE TRULY REVEALS its beauty when we grasp its intricate workings. I've come to understand that this understanding isn't something I can simply stumble upon; it's something that comes from embracing the peace of God. As the Scriptures say, "And the peace of God, which surpasses all understanding..." This peace is transformative. It grants me the ability to see beyond the flaws and shortcomings of others and perceive their deeper needs. It's through this peace that I find the strength to love my enemies, to extend forgiveness, and to show compassion even in the face of adversity. This peace isn't just a calm exterior; it's a profound inner tranquillity that enables me to navigate life's complexities with grace and understanding.

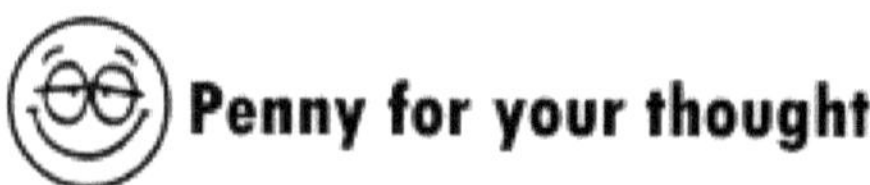

- What can we achieve when we cultivate and nurture the profound inner peace of God, allowing it to guide us in loving our enemies, extending forgiveness, and showing compassion during life's complications?

Love: Where can It be Found?

> Love was never lost to be found; it has always here within, waiting to be acknowledged and embraced

WHERE DOES LOVE RESIDE? Love, I've come to understand, isn't something external to seek out; it's a force within. It's the very essence of God, woven into the fabric of our being. When we embrace this truth, we realize that we carry love within us.

There's something special about tapping into this reservoir of love within ourselves. It's like unlocking a hidden treasure chest. As we let love flow from within, not only do we experience personal growth and fulfilment, but those around us also benefit. Our love becomes a catalyst for their growth and happiness.

So, rather than searching for love outside of ourselves, I've learned to turn inward. Love was never lost to be found; it has always here within, waiting to be acknowledged and embraced. When I started looking within, I found that love began to permeate every aspect of my life, transforming not just me but also the world around me.

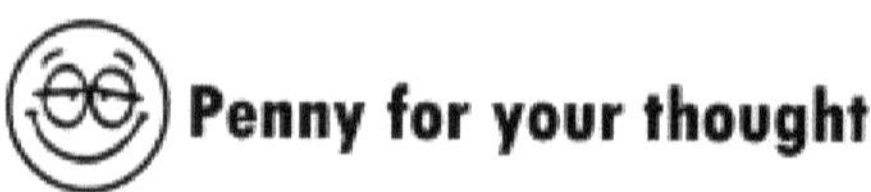

- Are you aware of the boundless reservoir of love within you?
- In what way can you allow this love to flow outward, enriching both your own life and the lives of those around us?

Wisdom

> "This prostitute of our emotions tends to appeal to our pain and anger, enticing us to follow paths that may not serve our best interests"

WHO IS THIS WAYWARD girl, this prostitute? My interpretation of this "Prostitute" is our very own emotions. Our desires, our initial responses to situations, are like the familiar paths we've learned since childhood. They're the feelings that often seek to comfort our hurts, shames, and pains. It's that inner voice urging us to retaliate or seek solace, akin to the call of a prostitute. Without knowledge and understanding, we risk being led astray by our emotions, which can obscure our judgment and cloud our hearts.

This prostitute of our emotions tends to appeal to our pain and anger, enticing us to follow paths that may not serve our best interests. Instead, the scriptures advise us to love wisdom as we would cherish a sweetheart. Just as a sweetheart refreshes our mind and brings joy, so too does understanding. We are encouraged to embrace wisdom intimately, to cling to her, and to nurture our relationship with understanding.

Penny for your thought

- What do understand about emotions and its influence on decisions making,
- How does prioritizing wisdom and understanding guide towards a path that serve your best interests?

Reflecting on Scriptures

BITS of Wisdom

Embracing God's Grace Despite Our Judgments

> God does not discard us because of our mistakes; in fact, He sees us through the lens of the purpose for which He created us.

READING THE BIBLE I find, sometimes, that I tend to be self-righteous. Once, I discovered this while reading about Samson in the Book of Judges. I found myself judging Samson harshly. I became angry at how he interacted with his parents. Such arrogance, evident in his every demands. I particularly took issue with his prayer having defeated a whole host of Philistine soldiers . In his prayer he seemed to accuse God of leaving him to die of thirst after a great victory. I was so angry, questioning whether the God I was reading about was the same God I served.

But God, in His consistency and mercy, spoke to me in a calm and comforting voice. He reminded me that our praises or criticisms of Him do not define who He is; He is God all by Himself. He assured me that He is not like man who would lie, and that He would continue to serve Samson, despite his snobbish attitude, so that his purpose may be fulfilled.

It has become clear to me than that God does not discard us because of our mistakes; in fact, He sees us through the lens of the purpose for which He created us. When God looks at us He sees purpose As the psalmist declared, "How precious are your thoughts towards me." This reassures us that no matter how many mistakes we make, God is not finished with us!

Let us, therefore, embrace His grace and goodness, living in the assurance that His love for us remains steadfast despite our shortcomings. May we learn to extend the same grace and compassion to others as we continue on our journey with the Lord.

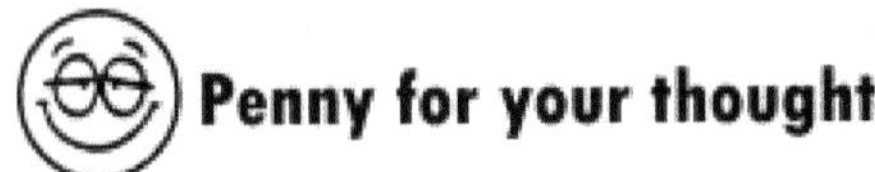

1. Have you ever caught yourself expecting God to fulfil your demands as if He were obligated to you?

Psalms 139:17-18

> God's thoughts towards us are grounded in the truth of our identity as His beloved children, created in His image and imbued with the breath of life

PSALMS 139:17-18 READS:

"How precious to me are your thoughts, God!
How vast is the sum of them!
Were I to count them,
they would outnumber the grains of sand—
when I awake, I am still with you."

As I revisit these verses, it's as though I'm offered a new lens through which to perceive God's boundless love for me. Contemplating the sheer magnitude of His thoughts leaves me humbled, grappling with the enormity of what love truly encompasses.

When I consider my own shortcomings and the ways I've fallen short, it's difficult to fathom what good thoughts God could harbour towards me. Yet, therein lies the beauty of His grace. His thoughts towards us transcend our actions and motives; they are rooted in His eternal intention and purpose for our lives.

Reflecting on the sacrificial love demonstrated on the cross, even when we were His enemies, reveals the depth of His unconditional love. It's a love that surpasses understanding, a love that saw beyond our flaws and recognized the inherent value bestowed upon us as His creation.

Indeed, God's thoughts towards us are grounded in the truth of our identity as His beloved children, created in His image and imbued with the breath of life. From the moment of our inception, His declaration of our worthiness echoed throughout eternity, unwavering and steadfast.

The challenge, then, becomes to align our thoughts with His divine perspective. Daily, I am compelled to ask myself: What are God's thoughts towards me, and can I embrace them as my own? Am I nurturing a mindset that reflects His love and grace towards myself and others?

In this journey of aligning our thoughts with God's, let us ponder these questions:

1. What are God's thoughts towards me?
2. Can I dwell in those thoughts, allowing them to shape my self-perception?
3. What are my thoughts towards myself, and do they align with God's truth?
4. Am I actively cultivating a mindset that mirrors His love and grace?
5. Whose thoughts am I embodying – my own, or those of my Creator?
6. Can I extend this same grace and love to others, cultivating positive thoughts towards them as well?

May we continually strive to embody the transformative power of God's thoughts, allowing His love to permeate every aspect of our lives and relationships.

Matthew 20:- The parable of the workers in the vineyard

> Are we mere robots to this world system?

EACH TIME I REVISIT this scripture, I find myself resonating with the frustration of the workers who laboured the entire day. I share their indignation and it ignites a similar fury within me. I can't help but explode with anger upon reading it, a reaction that repeats every single time I encounter this passage. How could those who worked such a short time receive the same pay as I do? But then, the landowner's words hit me: "Why are you angry? Is it because you are envious of my generosity?" Whoops. I hadn't considered that angle. I merely sensed an injustice, a hint of unfairness. But upon reflection, what's truly unfair about it? I agreed to work for a denarius, a day's wage. Now, I realize it might just be envy, or perhaps, a touch of jealousy.

In a real-life scenario, I find myself in a similar situation. "Why does this landowner favour those lazy workers over me?" I ponder. "How can he fail to recognize my hard work and offer me a raise, even a small one, while paying us all the same?" It's a shift from jealousy to selfishness. I failed to see from the beginning that the landowner aimed to provide everyone with an equal opportunity. But this feeling, it's undeniably real, deeply ingrained within us. Even when we can logically provide the correct answer, our habitual reactions tend to surface first—our true feelings.

So, how do we override these ingrained habits and develop a new response method? It's akin to fire drills, ensuring employees don't panic and jump out of windows during a fire. It's easy to say what we would or wouldn't do until we're actually faced with the situation. Peter confidently assured Jesus he wouldn't betray him, yet when tested, he did. Perhaps if he had some practice runs, things would have been different. There's prayer, yes, but there's also the need for practice. What should I practice, then?

We've inherited learned behaviours since birth, deeply rooted ways of doing things, even when they're not effective. We've become conditioned, defensive even, when questioned about these methods we've deemed as right. So, where do we begin to unlearn, relearn, and retrain our minds? Are we mere robots to this world system?

Penny for your thought

- What do you do when you are in a challenging situation where jealousy or selfishness dictate your reactions?

Barabbas and Me

> "I'll take his place" says a still small voice...

IN CHAINS I CAME, BOUND to death
my fears I tried, desperately to forget
How can I face them, what an embarrassment?
I am doomed! Today I am dead.
In just a few minutes, my name will be called
And there is no miracle that would free me at all
At least that what I thought

"I'LL TAKE HIS PLACE" says a still small voice
with such authority and power, calm and mild
I was lost for words and could only cry
For me?
Who would want to trade this place for me?
A wretched, self-centered, pigheaded sinner me.
"Yes" he said

I will take your chains for your freedom means much to me.

MY FREEDOM, I CANNOT brag
As a matter of fact, I am still taken aback.
Who is that guy that took my place?
I mean that much to him, I am still amaze
What could my freedom means to him?
I need to know, so that I can thank him.
He is my savior, I should make him my King
But embarrassingly I know nothing of him.
This will change, for if my freedom means much to him
Then it is my duty to know all about him.
His name is Jesus, the name they called
when they jeered, "Crucify him!"

I AM FOREVER GRATEFUL
Though I don't understand
But for this sake
and I will live!
In His Name

Penny for your thought

- How does the realization of Jesus sacrificing Himself for your freedom inspire you to learn more about him and deepen your relationship with them,

- How does this newfound freedom compel you to live differently?

A Mind Made Up

> "Your people shall be my people, and your God my God."

AS I DELVE INTO THE timeless narrative of Ruth and Naomi, I'm struck by the profound lessons hidden within its verses. It's easy to skim over the surface, focusing solely on Ruth's loyalty and Boaz's redemption. But as I pause to reflect, I find myself drawn to the character of Orpah, whose story often goes overlooked.

In the beginning, both Orpah and Ruth set out with Naomi on a journey to Israel. Their loyalty to their mother-in-law speaks volumes about the life she must have led—a life marked by love, kindness, and integrity. Yet, as they embarked on their homeward journey, Orpah hesitated. She weighed the options, assessed the situation, and ultimately chose to return to her homeland.

How often do we find ourselves in a similar position? We set out on a path, determined and resolute, only to falter at the first sign of adversity. Like Orpah, we may retreat to the safety of familiarity, clinging to old habits and comforts rather than embracing the unknown.

But Ruth's response reveals a different mindset—one characterized by unwavering determination and steadfast resolve. Despite Naomi's urging to return to her people and her gods, Ruth remained steadfast in her commitment. With a heart set on following Naomi, she declared, "Your people shall be my people, and your God my God."

Ruth's unwavering faith challenges us to examine our own convictions. Do we possess a made-up mind, firmly rooted in our beliefs and values? Or do we waver in the face of adversity, swayed by the shifting tides of circumstance?

As I ponder these questions, I'm reminded of the importance of representation. Just as Ruth saw something special in Naomi worth clinging to, others are watching us, observing how we represent ourselves, our families, our communities, and our faith. Are we living in a manner worthy of emulation, reflecting the light of Christ in all that we do?

Let us, therefore, bow our heads in prayer, seeking God's guidance and strength to cultivate a 'one-minded' mind—a mind that stands firm in the face of adversity, unwavering in its commitment to follow Christ. May we embrace the resources He has given us, using them wisely to bring glory to His name and further His kingdom here on earth.

Father, we thank You for Your wisdom and guidance. Help us to emulate the steadfast faith of Ruth, holding fast to Your promises even in the midst of uncertainty. Grant us the courage to represent You well in all that we do, that others may see Your light shining brightly through us. In Jesus' name, we pray. Amen.

Penny for your thought

- What caused Ruth to forsake her mother and father to follow Naomi?
- how does a person response to challenges reflect their commitment to their beliefs and values?

Linger a Little Longer

> "It was in her lingering that the truth unfolded before her eyes—the empty tomb was not a sign of loss but of resurrection and hope"

IMAGINE THE SCENE AT the empty tomb after the resurrection—the disciples, bewildered and uncertain, departing to their homes. Yet, there was Mary of Magdala, lingering at the graveside, her heart filled with questions and a longing to find her Lord.

Mary's decision to linger was no coincidence. In her stillness and persistence, she encountered the risen Christ, the one she had thought lost forever. It was in her lingering that the truth unfolded before her eyes—the empty tomb was not a sign of loss but of resurrection and hope.

Likewise, in our own lives, there is great value in lingering in the presence of Scripture. Rushing through passages may lead us to overlook the profound revelations waiting to be discovered. When we pause, reflect, and linger over the Word, its depths begin to unfold in ways that touch our hearts and transform our understanding.

Let us take a moment today to linger a little longer in Scripture. Instead of rushing through, let's dwell in its truths and mysteries. As we do, may the Holy Spirit unveil new insights and revelations, revealing the living Christ to us in ways that surpass our expectations.

May we be like Mary, willing to linger, seeking, and waiting upon the Lord. For it is in these moments of lingering that the profound truths of God's Word become deeply rooted in our hearts, guiding us closer to Him and His eternal truths.

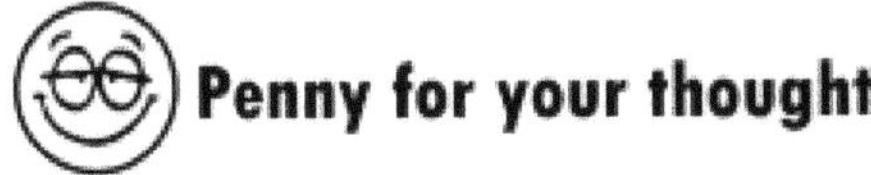

- Are there lessons to learn from Mary of Magdala's decision to linger at the empty tomb,

- how might the practice of lingering in Scripture deepen your understanding of God's truths and lead you closer to Him?

BITS of Wisdom

Embracing Unity in the Body of Christ

> "We are not meant to function in isolation but to rely on one another, just as different parts of a body work together for its survival and well-being. In this unity, we reflect God's love through Christ."

AS I REFLECT ON THE profound truth that we are the Body of Christ, I am struck by a realization—a realization that challenges my understanding of what it means to be part of this body.

Often, I have heard the phrase "we are the Body of Christ" and assumed it meant I am complete within myself. But the reality is quite different. To truly embody Christ's body means recognizing that I am just one part among many and to elaborate, a small fraction. Each of us are like individual cells or organs that contributes uniquely to the whole.

I wonder about the symbolism of Christ's body being broken. Could it be that His body was broken into tiny parts (bits) so that every human being in every corner of the world might receive a portion of Him? And when we believe and receive, then come together, the broken pieces of this body unite to form a complete representation of Christ on earth.

This realization underscores the importance of unity among believers. We are not meant to function in isolation but to rely on one another, just as different parts of a body work together for its survival and well-being. In this unity, we reflect God's love through Christ.

The passage that says, "By your love, they shall know me," takes on new depth when viewed through the lens of fellowship and unity within the Body of Christ. Love here is more than a feeling—it's the tangible expression of our fellowship and interconnectedness. It's through our coming together in unity that we uniquely and perfectly display the essence of Christ to the world.

Let us embrace this truth today—that we are interconnected parts of Christ's body, each with a vital role to play. As we cultivate love and unity among believers, we not only strengthen ourselves but also reveal Christ's presence and character to a world in need of His light. May our fellowship be a beacon of hope and a testimony to the transformative power of Christ's love within us.

Penny for your thought

- How can your fellowship with other believers serve as a beacon of hope to those outside the Body of Christ
- Reflect on the idea that we are interconnected parts of Christ's body. How does this understanding influence your daily actions and interactions with others?

Nurturing Through Understanding: The Essence of Care

> "To truly serve, we must first understand and acknowledge where others are in their journey"

SERVICE TO OTHERS ACTS as a mirror, revealing the true state of your heart. Through our interactions with others, we may realize the importance of a fundamental shift in our approach—a transformation rooted in empathy and genuine care. Too often, we find yourself frustrated when people don't meet our expectations or follow the path we envisioned for them. In hindsight, we see that your motives were driven by our own agenda rather than a sincere desire to support and empower. How can we claim to serve others' needs when our focus remains fixed solely on our objectives?

To truly serve, we must first understand and acknowledge where others are in their journey. Their experiences, struggles, and aspirations deserve recognition and empathy. It's about embracing them for who they are and meeting them at their point of need, rather than imposing our own agenda.

Just as aiming an arrow requires a clear understanding of both the starting point and the target, so too does nurturing relationships. By taking the time to empathize and truly listen without judgment, we can gain insight into others' needs and aspirations. This understanding forms the foundation upon which genuine care and support can be built.

At the core of it all lies love—a love that transcends expectations and embraces individuals for who they are. It's through this lens of love that we should endeavour to nurture and support those around you, recognizing that true care begins with understanding and acceptance.

May we strive to serve others with a heart full of empathy, understanding, and unconditional love, reflecting the heart of Christ in your actions and relationships.

Penny for your thought

- Have you ever find yourself serving for the sake of your agenda?
- How can you shift your approach to service from one driven by personal agendas to one rooted in empathy, and genuine care for others' needs and aspirations?

Navigating the sea of life

> "when we aren't adequately prepared for the challenges of life, we tend to blame others"

DRAWING A PARALLEL between our lives and a boat at sea, it's clear that preparation is key to navigating the waters successfully. A seasoned sailor ensures that their vessel meets all necessary requirements before setting sail, allowing them to traverse the seas with confidence. They don't waste time blaming external factors like storms, wind, or waves for any mishaps.

Similarly, when we aren't adequately prepared for the challenges of life, we tend to blame others. Our upbringing may resemble the various elements of nature—a parent could be the guiding wind, other family members and neighbours the tumultuous storm, and teachers and school the relentless waves. These childhood experiences often shape our self-esteem, confidence, and ability to live purposefully as adults.

But now, as adults, we have the power to steer our own ships. We can transform past struggles into newfound purpose, much like a sailor prepares themselves for a voyage. Just as a sailor equips themselves for the sea, we too can prepare ourselves for life's challenges.

So, what do we need to do? First, we must identify the deficiencies from our childhood—low self-esteem, lack of support, and insufficient celebration of achievements, among others. Then, we can start by cultivating self-awareness, using the mirror as a tool for introspection.

By looking into our own eyes, we confront ourselves with truth and honesty. We can apologize to ourselves for neglecting our true selves and not showing enough love and appreciation. We can also express gratitude for our resilience, kindness, and love towards others.

Furthermore, we can spend quality time with ourselves, getting to know our thoughts and feelings. This emotional preparation equips us to navigate life's challenges with grace and resilience, much like a prepared sailor can navigate the winds and storms at sea.

Ultimately, when we're emotionally equipped, we no longer need to blame external circumstances for our struggles. Instead, we can respond to life's challenges with kindness and respect, knowing that we have the strength and resilience to overcome them.

Penny for your thought

- In what ways can you begin to equip yourself emotionally today to navigate the challenges you face?

Beauty Beyond the Surface

> "God's delight in us stems not from our outward appearance but from our ability to fulfil the purposes He has ordained for us."

IN A WORLD FIXATED on appearances, it's easy to believe that our outward presentation defines our worth and purpose. From the meticulously groomed individuals to the carefully curated social media feeds, the emphasis on external beauty can feel overwhelming, shaping our perceptions of ourselves and others.

Yet, beneath the surface lies a deeper truth—a truth echoed in the realm of programming, where functionality takes precedence over aesthetics. Just as a programmer meticulously crafts a program to execute specific tasks, so too does God intricately design each of us with a purpose in mind.

In the world of coding, beauty is found not in flashy designs but in flawless execution. Similarly, God's delight in us stems not from our outward appearance but from our ability to fulfil the purposes He has ordained for us. Just as a program relies on its housing to function effectively, our earthly bodies serve as vessels for our spiritual beings, intertwined and interdependent.

When God formed us in His image, He fashioned us for functionality, not for superficial beauty contests. He peers beyond the surface, delving into the depths of our hearts to discern our true essence. For Him, it is the inward qualities—the kindness, love, and faithfulness—that hold significance.

Consider the profound implications of our existence. Just as a programmer imbues a computer with a portion of their mind, so too has God endowed us with a fragment of His divine essence. Could it be that He expects us to operate in alignment with His design, fulfilling the purposes He has uniquely ordained for each of us?

As we navigate the complexities of life, let us ponder our true identity and purpose. Let us not be swayed by the world's shallow standards but instead seek to understand the depth of God's intentions for us. For in realizing our true selves, we unlock the potential to fulfil His divine plan with humility and purpose.

Reflect on the correlation between the house and the program. Just as a computer interprets instructions to communicate intelligibly, so too are we called to decipher God's guidance and manifest His wisdom in our lives. Let us engage in dialogue, sharing our insights and ponderings as we journey together towards a deeper understanding of ourselves and our Creator.

Food for thought indeed. Let us continue to explore these profound mysteries, seeking illumination and inspiration in the boundless depths of God's wisdom.

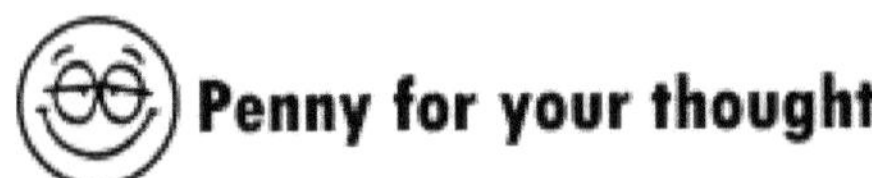

- How can you shift your focus from outward appearances to the inward qualities?
- Can you identify your inward qualities that truly define your worth and purpose?
- In what way can you align your life with God's unique design for you?

Leaving a Legacy: Life Between Birth and Death:

> We must be deliberate and intentional in our living

IN THE JOURNEY BETWEEN birth and death lies the essence of living. We are given the precious gift of breath at birth, and it is eventually taken away at death. But it is in the process of living that we truly leave our mark, our legacy.

Each day, we have the opportunity to ponder the legacy we are leaving behind. Whose lives are we touching? Whose spirits are we uplifting with the breath of life that emanates from us? It's essential to reflect on the impact we are making daily and whether it aligns with the legacy we wish to leave.

While we are not responsible for the circumstances of our birth or the timing of our death, we are entirely accountable for the way we live our lives. We shape our legacy through our choices, actions, and interactions with others.

Consider the breath given to us as an investment from our Creator, entrusted to us to live purposefully and intentionally. Just as a wise investor evaluates their investments, we too must assess how we are utilizing the breath of life given to us.

Living for the glory of God means making decisions that align with His will and bring honour to His name. It's about using our gifts and talents not for selfish gain but to glorify God and bless others.

We must be deliberate and intentional in our living, recognizing that every decision we make contributes to the legacy we leave behind. Whether we live spiritually, situationally, or selfishly will determine the impact we have on the world around us.

Living spiritually involves aligning our lives with God's purposes, seeking to honour Him in all that we do. It's about trusting Him with our plans and allowing His wisdom to guide our steps.

Living situationally or selfishly may lead to conflicting legacies and uncertain impacts on others. It's essential to consider how our actions affect those around us and strive to leave a positive imprint on the world.

As we navigate the journey of life, let us remember that we are accountable for how we live each day. Let us strive to leave a legacy of love, kindness, and compassion, breathing the breath of life into those we encounter.

May we live with purpose, intentionality, and a deep desire to honour God in all that we do. And may our legacy be one that reflects His grace, mercy, and unfailing love for all humanity.

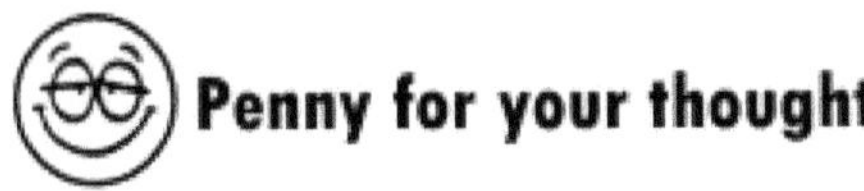

AS YOU REFLECT ON THE legacy you are building with each breath and action, consider these:

- How am I intentionally shaping my daily choices to ensure

that my legacy aligns with the purpose and honour of God,

- How am I leaving a lasting impact of love, kindness, and compassion on the world around me?

Lord, Teach Me to Love You Right

> "Love, not just as a feeling, but as sacrifice, service, and responsibility."

LIKE PETER, I'VE FOUND myself in moments where I denied Jesus—not always with words, but through my actions, my silence, or my failure to stand for Him. Each time, guilt would flood in, and I'd become my own harshest critic. Deep down, I knew I loved Him, yet I was failing miserably to live out that love out with boldness and consistency.

So, I began a personal journey—asking hard questions. Why did Peter deny Jesus? I truly believe Peter loved Him and would have done anything for Him. But when I studied John 21:16-19, I started to see Peter's denial in a new light. Before Jesus' crucifixion and resurrection, Peter loved Jesus with a kind of love many of us start with—a surface-level, emotional, self-assured love shaped more by the world than by God. It was the kind of love that feels strong in comfort but crumbles under pressure.

I don't think Jesus could've asked Peter, "Do you love me?" three times before the crucifixion—Peter wouldn't have heard him. His confidence in himself was too loud. But after the resurrection, something had changed. Peter had been broken and humbled. His response came from a place of self-awareness and Jesus, in that moment, revealed what true love looks like: Feed my lambs. Take care of my sheep. Love, not just as a feeling, but as a sacrifice, service, and responsibility.

Peter's eagerness to jump out of the boat and run to Jesus when he heard He was on the shore—that was more than excitement. I believe it was a desperate longing to reclaim and embrace the love he thought he had lost.

So when Jesus asks, "Do you love me?"—He's not asking if we feel affectionate toward Him or if we're willing to do good things when it's convenient. He's asking if we're willing to give up our lives for Him, to love the way He loves.

That hit me hard. I realized that in my own life, I was loving Jesus in convenient ways—doing things I assumed would please Him, but on my terms. And that's why I kept denying Him in the harder moments.

Now, instead of beating myself up, I've started to pray: Lord, help me to love You the way You love me.

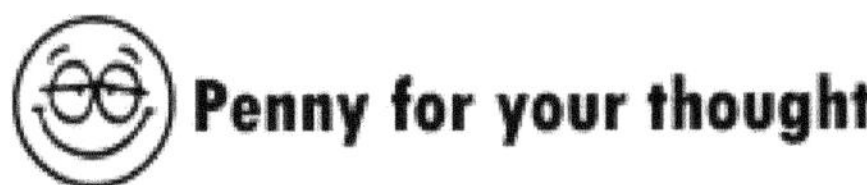

- When Jesus asks you, "Do you love me?", how would you honestly respond?
- What would it look like for you to "feed His sheep" in your current season of life?
- Have you been doing things for Jesus that are convenient—or are you letting Him lead you into deeper love and service?
- What step can you take today to move from guilt to grace—to stop beating yourself up and start walking in love?

Shine Your Light

> "Life has shown me that some with knowledge often dim their light, standing in the shadows of bold individuals."

DO NOT HIDE YOUR LIGHT under a bushel. Be the radiant light that God created you to be, and never diminish it to become a shadow for someone else.

As I observed the people who seemed to be advancing in life, I realized that their success wasn't necessarily due to their superior knowledge, but often because they were bold enough to take steps forward. Life has shown me that some with knowledge often dim their light, standing in the shadows of bold individuals.

Many of us are timid and shy, speaking only in small groups, using conversation as an outlet rather than a means to action. In these small circles, much talk happens, but little is done. On the other hand, the bold person steps out, willing to learn and grow, even at the risk of ridicule.

In this fast-paced world, where everyone is striving to find their place, it is crucial to recognize the light within each of us. When you find yourself living as a shadow, remember that God has given you a unique light to shine. Be bold and step out. Yes, you might be laughed at or criticized, but that is far better than living a life in the shadows. Living as a shadow means you are not truly living.

Being ridiculed is an opportunity for growth. It teaches us to try again, to learn from our experiences, and to adjust our light accordingly. Be bold, be bright, and let your light shine. There are circumstances that need your light, people who will learn from it, and others who draw energy from it.

When you feel down, it's okay to dim your light temporarily, but never let it go out completely. Remember, your light is a gift from God, meant to illuminate the path for yourself and others. So, step out of the shadows, embrace your divine light, and shine brightly. The world needs your light.

Penny for your thought

- How can you support and encourage others to let their lights shine brightly?
- Reflect on the times you have felt down. What helped you to keep your light from going out completely?
- What are some practical steps you can take to embrace your divine light and shine brightly in challenging circumstances?

Confronting Our Past with Truth and Grace

> "Our past has a way of catching up with us and causing the same damage if we are not prepared to deal with it."

WE CANNOT HIDE, BURY, run from, or ignore our past. It is imperative that we stand up to our past, accept it, and overcome it so that we can move forward. Our past has a way of catching up with us and causing the same damage if we are not prepared to deal with it. No matter how fast or far we have run, it has a tendency to show up unexpectedly and uninvited. Even if we bury it deep, it finds a way to resurface.

The truth is, if our past is not overcome, it can affect our present decisions, which, in turn, may affect our loved ones and potentially cause greater damage than we deserve. So, how do we deal with our past, whether it haunts us, or we don't even remember it? We begin with the truth.

Acknowledge that it has already happened. If you feel unequipped to handle the magnitude of the situation, seek professional help. Otherwise, find a quiet place and replay the situation as it is. Try not to create interpretations or justifications. Acknowledge your feelings toward the situation and allow them to run their course. Do not justify, rationalize, or interpret; simply let them be.

Give yourself time to grieve if necessary. Forgive all parties involved, including yourself, and ask God for the grace to move forward and leave it behind. By confronting our past with truth and grace, we can find healing and freedom to live fully in the present and embrace the future with hope.

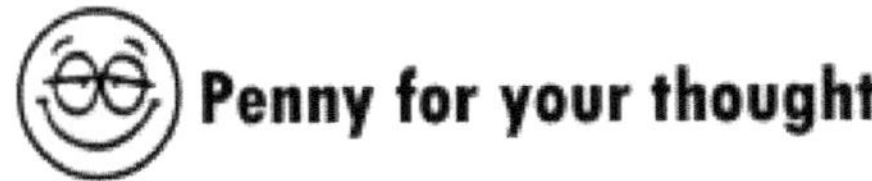

- How can you balance accepting your past while also focusing on personal growth and future aspirations?
- Reflect on the importance of acknowledging the truth of your past experiences. How does this step pave the way for genuine healing and transformation?
- Reflect on a moment from your past that you have tried to hide, bury, or run from. How has it impacted your present life?
- Why do you think it is important to stand up to and accept your past in order to move forward?

The Original Author: Don't Forget to Cite Him

> “God breathes life into us daily. He gifts us with talents, ideas, creativity, and purpose”

HAVE YOU NOTICED HOW often copyright comes up these days? Whether it's music, videos, books, or social media posts—giving credit to the original creator has become a big deal. People are becoming more aware of the need to acknowledge someone else's work, and if they don't, there are consequences.

Here's a though, what about the ultimate Creator? The One who authored the heavens, the earth, and life itself? How often do we stop to give Him credit?

God breathes life into us daily. He gifts us with talents, ideas, creativity, and purpose. Yet we can go days, even weeks, without acknowledging Him as the source.

Still, He's gracious. He gently nudges us back with reminders in everyday life, through beauty in nature, through answered prayer, through a whisper in our spirit that says, “Don't forget who wrote your story.”.

Let's not wait for a crisis or correction to remember the Author of it all. Cite HIM!

Penny for your thought

- Am I giving God the credit He deserves for the life, talents, and opportunities I've been given?

Living with Eyes Up

> "When we truly grasp this reality, it changes how we live."

HAVE YOU EVER FOUND yourself adjusting your behavior the moment you realized someone was watching? Maybe you sat up straighter, chose your words more carefully, or avoided doing something questionable. There's just something about being seen that naturally shifts how we act.

Now imagine if we brought that same kind of awareness into our everyday lives—not just occasionally, but consistently. What if we lived with the conscious understanding that we are always seen—not only in our actions, but in our thoughts and motives?

But here's the beautiful difference: the One watching us isn't looking to catch us in a mistake. He's not waiting to point fingers or shame us. He's a loving Father who wants to guide us, shape us, and help us walk in the path of right living.

When we truly grasp this reality, it changes how we live. We begin to see God not as a harsh judge, but as the gentle, patient Father who sees us fully, loves us completely, and walks with us faithfully.

He's not waiting for us to stumble so He can punish us—He's waiting for us to look up, to notice Him, to trust Him, and to follow His lead.

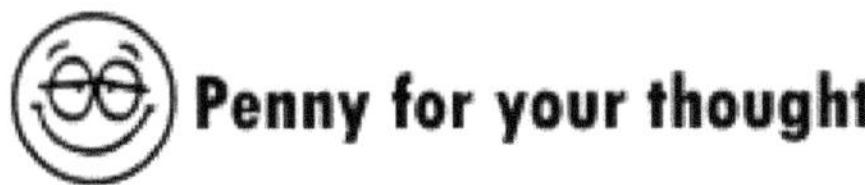

- Do I live each day as though my words, thoughts, and actions are being recorded—not for punishment, but for purpose?
- What everyday moments might God be using to get my attention right now?
- How would my choices change if I truly lived with an awareness of God's loving presence watching over me?

Footprints That Last

> "What if we viewed each day the way we view our digital platforms?"

IN TODAY'S DIGITAL age, everything we share—every photo, post, and comment—leaves a lasting mark. Our digital footprints tell a story. They shape how others see us, and in some cases, they follow us for years.

But there's an even greater trail we're leaving behind: our spiritual footprint.

Every word we speak, every action we take, every thought we entertain—whether public or private—leaves a mark. It's not hidden from God. It's not forgotten. In fact, it's shaping something far bigger than our online presence. It's shaping our character, our witness, and the legacy we leave behind.

What if we viewed each day the way we view our digital platforms—understanding that what we say and do is not temporary, but eternal? That nothing is wasted? That every choice we make has a ripple effect, reaching beyond ourselves to our children, and even our children's children?

That perspective changes things. It causes us to pause. To be more intentional. To live not just as good digital citizens—but as faithful earthly citizens preparing for a greater Kingdom to come.

As our digital lives affect our earthly reputations, our earthly lives impact our eternal futures.

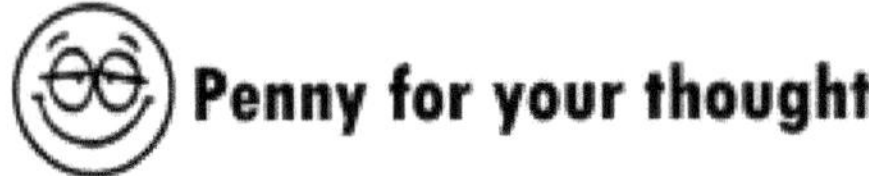

- If my life were a digital footprint, what story would it tell about my relationship with God?

Embrace the Process of Growth

> "every step in our own growth journey prepares us for the platform where we will fulfil our purpose."

GROWTH CANNOT BE RUSHED. Every stage of growth is necessary for the next phase and ultimately, the destination. It is futile to attempt to reach the end of the growth process without undergoing the necessary development.

Consider the analogy of fruit. Each stage of growth prepares the fruit to become full and flavourful. Similarly, birds strengthen their beaks and wings through gradual growth, which is essential for their survival. Likewise, every step in our own growth journey prepares us for the platform where we will fulfil our purpose.

A rush to the platform can be detrimental, both to ourselves and those around us. Taking the time to learn and develop allows us to master our skills and talents, enabling us to produce effectively and efficiently on our designated platform.

Let us embrace the process of growth, trusting that each step is essential for our ultimate fulfilment. May we cultivate patience and perseverance, recognizing that growth cannot be hurried, but must be nurtured and allowed to unfold in its own time.

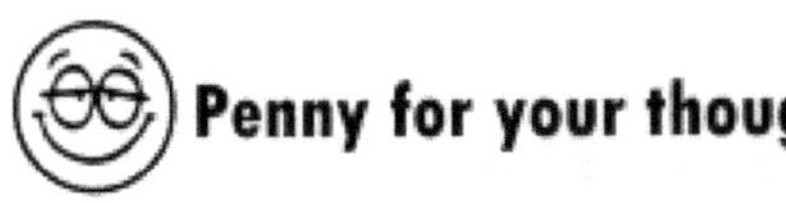

- How do you handle setbacks or slow progress in your growth journey? What strategies help you stay motivated?
- In what ways can you nurture your growth process to ensure it unfolds naturally?
- How do you understand the analogy of fruit growing and birds strengthening their beaks and wings in relation to your own growth?

Gratitude Clears Our Vision

> “In world where all should be going wrong, let’s thank God, things are going right!”

UNGRATEFULNESS CAN impair our spiritual vision, blinding us to the possibilities and goodness that God has placed before us. When we become ungrateful, our focus shifts to the wrongs done to us and by us, clouding our sight and leaving us blind to God's blessings. This is evident all around us, as we constantly find someone to blame—parents, pastors, politicians, society, the system—just about everybody and everything.

The truth is, there is always another side to the story, and something good is always happening. We often hear, "How can a good God let bad things happen?" Let's change this narrative: because God is good, He brings good out of bad situations. In world where all should be going wrong, let's thank God, things are going right! Ungratefulness, corrodes our spiritual eyes, causing us to miss the goodness of God that is continually pursuing us. Often, our negative feelings are simply clouding our perception.

Let us look for the hand of God in all situations and praise Him for who He is—a good God who relentlessly chases us with His goodness.

In this fallen world, where things can go wrong, I encounter good because God is here. Instead of allowing ungratefulness to blur our vision, let us open our eyes to see God's endless grace and mercy. Thankfulness restores our sight, enabling us to witness and celebrate God's unwavering love and presence in our lives.

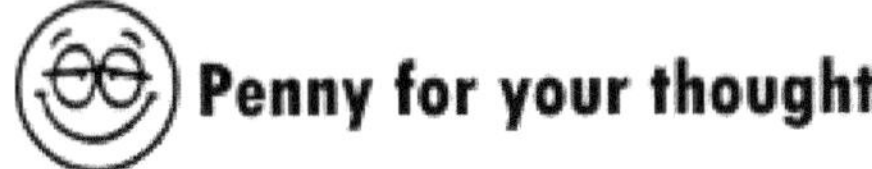

- What practical steps can you take to cultivate gratitude in your daily life?
- What steps can you take to prevent ungratefulness from blurring your spiritual vision in the future?
- Reflect on the idea that in a fallen world, good things still happen because of God's presence. How does this influence your understanding of God's character?

Don't miss out!

Visit the website below and you can sign up to receive emails whenever Nathlee R. Grant publishes a new book. There's no charge and no obligation.

https://books2read.com/r/B-A-WKVEB-OANBD

BOOKS 2 READ

Connecting independent readers to independent writers.

Did you love *Bits and Bites of Truth and Wisdom*? Then you should read *Breaking Chains: A Mother's Journey to Healing and Redemption*[1] by Nathlee R. Grant and Nathlee R. Grant!

[2]

"Stop that you stupid child. Why would you even do that? You are just like my mother!" Angry words often slip from the lips of angry parents, but I posit that there is fuel deeper than anger which often breaks the bonds between mother and child. Come journey with me on a path to deliverance from the unseen beast of Emotional Abuse.

---

1. https://books2read.com/u/ml61xB

2. https://books2read.com/u/ml61xB

Also by Nathlee R. Grant

Breaking Chains: A Mother's Journey to Healing and Redemption
Bits and Bites of Truth and Wisdom

About the Author

Ms. Nathlee Grant has spent nearly 30 years in community development and in recent times focused particularly on developing and maintaining healthy parent-child relationships. She has launched numerous initiatives in this regard which never took off as expected, but boasted successes, nonetheless. These include formal sessions such as 'Youth and Adults Time 2 Talk', 'Teens Wise Up and Rise' and 'Who Am I'. Informally, Nathlee has advised many parents and even assisted in strengthening, encouraging and preserving their parent-child relationship.

In this newfound zeal of hers Ms. Grant has entered the whole new world of education completing her Post Graduate Diploma in Education and Training, graduating as valedictorian in 2022, and pursuing another Post Graduate Diploma in Learning Technologies simultaneously with a Master of Science Degree in Education and Leadership.

Moreover, Ms. Grant has interacted and built rapport with teens from many varied backgrounds through academic assistance. Furthermore, Ms. Grant has contributed to her son's school by advising frustrated parents, teachers and students and has remained among the best known and loved parents in his age group. She also stands respected in her family as a fountain of wisdom and a pioneer of change.

This book, years in the making, serves as her testament to the power of God and the power of change that can be made evident in every household, if every parent will allow it. If God changed an angry, emotionally abusive teenage mom, He can change you too!

www.ingramcontent.com/pod-product-compliance
Ingram Content Group UK Ltd.
Pitfield, Milton Keynes, MK11 3LW, UK
UKHW021656190726
13853UKWH00001B/300